Building Jewish Identity **4**

JEWISH HISTORY AND HERITAGE

By Judy Dick

BEHRMAN HOUSE
www.behrmanhouse.com

Fictional narratives on pages 8, 16, 22, 28, 34, 40 by Mark H. Levine

Design: Anne Redmond Design
Series design: Terry Taylor Studio
Editor: Dena Neusner
Editorial consultants: Ellen J. Rank, Diane Zimmerman
Map illustration on page 13: Jim McMahon

Copyright © 2013 Behrman House, Inc.
Published by Behrman House, Inc.
Springfield, NJ 07081
www.behrmanhouse.com

ISBN: 978-0-87441-867-5
Printed in the United States of America

To my global family, hailing from
America and England, Belgium and Israel, from
whom I learn Jewish history firsthand.

—Judy Dick

The publisher wishes to acknowledge the following sources for quotes:
Quoted portion of narrative page 16: *The Special Laws*, by Philo of Alexandria
Quoted portion of narrative page 22: *Diwan* by medieval poet Samuel Ha'Nagid
Quoted portion of narrative page 34: Abe Cahan in *Finding the Jewish Shakespeare: The Life and Legacy of Jacob Gordin,* Syracuse University Press, 2007
First quoted portion of narrative page 40: *Shomrim* slogan, from a poem by Ya'akov Cahan, 1903
Second quoted portion of narrative page 40: Maurice Samuel, *Harvest in the Desert.* Knopf, 1945
Excerpt on page 25: from *Cairo Genizah*, translation by Goitein, S. D., from Gerard Nahon and Charles Touati, eds. *Hommage à Georges Vajda: études d'histoire et pensé juives.* Peeters, 1980
Excerpt on page 33: *The Memoirs of Glückel of Hameln,* Schocken Books, 1977
Excerpt on page 47: from Judea and Ruth Pearl, ed. *I Am Jewish: Personal Reflections Inspired by the Last Words of Daniel Pearl,* Jewish Lights, 2005

The publisher gratefully acknowledges the following sources of photographs and graphic images:
(T=top, B=bottom, L=left, R=right)
Art Resource: Scala 36B; Bigstock: Nadin 48; Cambridge University Library 24B; Felix Nussbaum Haus 43MR; Gila Gevirtz 17; Israel Post 31B; Israeli Government Press Office: 41, Zoltan Kluger 44L, Teddy Brauner (Iraqis) 44BL, Nathan Alpert 44BR; Israeli Ministry of Tourism www.golsrael.com 45B; Levi Strauss & Co. Archives San Francisco 35; Reuters: Brian Synder 46; Richard Nowitz Photography (cover main photo, 1); Shutterstock: AISPIX by Image Source (cover Torah), Margot Petrowski (cover kids), Nuno Andre (cover flag), Barna Tanko (cover bagels), Samuel Perry (cover menorah), Kiselev Andrey Valerevich 2-3, Alex and Anna (map) 4-5 and 31, Luciano Mortula (statue) 4, Chiyacat 5TM, Elzbieta Sekowska 5TR, Andrea Skjold 5 BM, picsfive 6T, Eugene Ivanov 6BL, ChaemeleonsEye 6BR, Butterfly Hunter 7T, wjarek 7BM, Rozhkovs 7BR, pandapaw 8M, Shpringel Olga 8BR, artform 8L, Darrell J. Rohl 9, Vietrov Dmytro 11, blueeyes 12T, Maximus256 12R, kavram 14R, SergiyN 15T, Aleksandar Mijatovic 15M, pandapaw 16M, Seleznev Oleg 16B, blueeyes 18T, holbox 20TL, Roman Sigaev 20BR, silver-john 22M, Petrafler 22B, Monkey Business Images 27, wanchai 28M, Lusoimages 28L, Odelia Cohen 28R, Johannes Wiebel 32, photostudio7 34M, Ruslan Kudrin 34R, leonello calvetti 36T, studioVin (books) 37T, koya979 (notes) 37M, Kostyantyn Ivanyshen (ship) 37M, Keith Levit (tallit) 38T, Ussr79 (sewing machine) 38T, pavelr (candlesticks) 38T, Vereshchagin Dmitry (violin) 38T, Pavel K (music clef) 38T, Leah613 (tzedakah box) 38T, Charles Shapiro (dreidel) 38T, cloki (trunk) 38-39T, VectorZilla 38B, Volodymyr Burdiak (stopwatch) 39T, Eduardo Ramirez Sanchez (kippah) 39T, Howard Sandler (Torah) 39T, S1001 (challah) 39T, BrAt82 40, Mikhail 45R, Iakov Filimonov 47; Trustees of the British Museum 20BL; Wikimedia Commons: perwinklekog 4L, 1671 painting 4BR, painting by Henry Alexander Ogden 5TL, Almog 5BL, stringparts 5BR, 7BL, 10, 13T, 14L, Guillaume Rouille 1553 18BL, 18BR, from Codex Manesse 23, 24T, 24L, 26, detail from The Rothschild Miscellany 29, Miguel Angel "fotografo" 30T, Fisherjs 30B, Jewish Encyclopedia 33, 37B, Jonsafari (siddur) 39T, 39B, 42-43B, 43T, Daniel Ullrich 43ML.

Library of Congress Cataloging-in-Publication Data
Dick, Judy.
  Jewish history and heritage / by Judy Dick.
      pages cm. -- (Building Jewish identity ; 4)
  ISBN 978-0-87441-867-5
  1. Jews--History--Juvenile literature. 2. Jews--History--Textbooks for children. I. Title.
  DS118.D533 2013
  909'.04924--dc23
                        2012047979

CONTENTS

CHAPTER 1

WELCOME TO YOUR WORLD

Our World at a Glance: Jewish Life in America

From bagels to blue jeans, matzah ball soup to the Magen David symbol, Jews have contributed to American culture in many ways. Did you know that a Jewish American poet wrote the famous poem that's inscribed on the Statue of Liberty? Or that a Jewish American doctor invented the vaccine that wiped out the crippling disease polio? Or that a Jewish American songwriter wrote the famous song "God Bless America"? Similarly, your life is shaped by all the American Jews who came before you. Many came from places around the globe and introduced new ideas to the American scene. Exploring their history helps us understand our world today.

NORTH AMERICA

Canada

You can find both French and English speakers in the Jewish communities of Canada, most of whom live in Montreal or Toronto. This Canadian synagogue is the oldest on the west coast of North America.

United States

"Give me your tired, your poor, your huddled masses yearning to breathe free…" These words by the Jewish poet Emma Lazarus grace the Statue of Liberty, which has welcomed countless immigrants to the United States.

SOUTH AMERICA

Brazil

The first Jews in North America came from Brazil in 1654 and settled in New Amsterdam (now New York City).

Did You Know...

Famous Jewish Americans include Albert Einstein, Harry Houdini, Maurice Sendak, and Barbara Streisand.

Germany

Jewish immigrants from Germany introduced Reform congregations, department stores, and even blue jeans to the United States.

England

During the American Revolution, many Jewish immigrants from England fought for America, against the British.

Eastern Europe: Poland and Russia

Jewish immigrants from Eastern Europe introduced Americans to popular Ashkenazic treats like challah, bagels, blintzes, and matzah balls.

ASIA

EUROPE

Iran

Iranian Jews fleeing the Islamic Revolution built a community in Los Angeles, California. There you can hear people speaking the Persian language Farsi and taste Persian stews.

AFRICA

AUSTRALIA

Morocco

Moroccan Jews brought with them to Montreal, Canada, their day-after-Passover holiday, the Mimouna, during which they return to eating leavened bread.

Israel

The American Jewish community shares a unique friendship with Israel, the tiny country that is home to nearly half of the world's Jewish population. Many American and Israeli Jews share family ties, a commitment to Jewish culture, and a love of falafel and hummus.

Jewish History in My Life

How did the American Jewish community become so diverse? Why do most Jews in the world live in the United States or Israel? Studying Jewish history gives us answers to these and many more questions. Jewish history is the story of *Am Yisrael,* the Jewish people, and how our ancestors defined their Jewish identity as they faced changing times and moved to new places around the world. What questions do you have about your Jewish community?

Connecting across the Centuries

If Jews from the past, like the biblical Miriam or Hillel the sage, stepped into your world today, they would likely not recognize much of modern Jewish life. But there would be some things they could identify because Jewish tradition has been handed down from one generation to the next for thousands of years. Jewish history is like a chain, and each generation is a link in the chain connecting all Jews across time.

Building on the Past

The story of the most popular Jewish symbol, the menorah, is just one example of how Jewish life today is built upon our rich history:

1. The seven-branched gold menorah, described in detail in the Torah, was one of the holy objects our ancestors created in the desert after the Exodus from Egypt and carried with them into Israel.

2. A menorah was used in the First and Second Temples in Jerusalem. When the Maccabees regained control of the Temple from the Greeks and lit the menorah, it became a symbol of Jewish resistance. We remember this miracle on Ḥanukkah when we light the eight-branched Ḥanukkah menorah.

My Jewish Story

Add a page to Jewish history by writing your personal story. Write what you know about your family's history and origins. Describe any Jewish objects, values, traditions, foods, or even names that have been handed down to you from someone in your family.

Talk about It

How can studying Jewish history help you understand your own family's past?

My Jewish Story

3. A detail from the famous Arch of Titus in Rome, Italy, shows an image of the menorah being taken by the Romans after they destroyed the Second Temple.

4. For centuries, Jews have included the menorah symbol on ritual objects and in synagogue art, such as this decoration from a historic synagogue in Krakow, Poland.

5. Finally, the menorah came full circle when it was chosen to be the main symbol on modern Israel's state emblem.

The travels of the menorah parallel that of Am Yisrael. Like the menorah, the Jewish people started a new life in the desert, had their glory days in their home in Israel, and were exiled, forced to leave Israel and find new homes around the world. Like the menorah symbol, Am Yisrael returned home when the modern state of Israel was established. Jewish history illustrates these repeated themes of exile and return. It is the story of how the Jewish people kept the *Brit*, our covenant with God, both in Israel and in the Diaspora, the many Jewish communities outside of Israel that were built as Jews moved farther and farther across the world. You are part of the newest chapter of Jewish history.

CHAPTER 2

BIBLICAL TIMES: BECOMING AM YISRAEL

Dear Diary,

I'm terrified, though my parents tell me not to worry. They say everything will be all right, but how do they know? Nothing like this has happened before; it feels as if nature is out of control. The other day, swarms of insects swooped down on the Egyptians. I could hear children and adults crying as they pleaded to their gods for help. It became so unbearable that I covered my ears, but I couldn't turn off my imagination. My mind pictured insects crawling over the Egyptians.

But nothing so far has been as frightening as the wall of blackness that inched its way across the sky today. Within minutes it had swallowed the sun, and the land of Egypt, except where we live, was completely dark. Moses says that God is angry at Pharaoh, and that the Holy One has sent these plagues to free us. I hope it's true. Life is miserable in slavery. No one is safe from the taskmasters' whips.

My father believes that if Pharaoh won't free us, there will be one more plague, and then Pharaoh will change his mind. Everyone is getting ready to leave. Like our neighbors, we've slaughtered a lamb and smeared its blood on our doorposts to ward off something terrible. My mother is roasting the meat for a feast tonight. I'm not sure what will happen, but I'm excited. They're calling me now...I must go.

Rachel
Goshen, Egypt

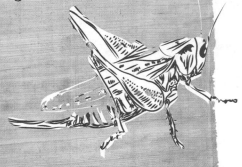

KEY EVENTS

About 1300 BCE	About 1000 BCE	About 950 BCE	About 928 BCE
Joshua leads the Israelites to conquer the Land of Israel	David becomes the second king of Israel	King Solomon begins building the First Temple	Israel divided into two kingdoms, Israel and Judah

Laying a Foundation

From ancient Egypt to the Land of Israel, Babylonia to Poland, Am Yisrael held onto its unique identity throughout the centuries, not forgetting its history or values. Just as you have a unique identity, every nation has one too, and its early history gives us a clue about its values.

Consider the early history of Am Yisrael, starting with the dynamic duo, Abraham and Sarah. They first set foot in Canaan, the future Jewish homeland, around 4,000 years ago, and forged the original Brit with God. Pivotal events like the Exodus from Egypt, receiving the Torah, and entering the Land of Israel are part of the history that is the foundation of Am Yisrael's identity. At every point of Am Yisrael's early life, great personalities helped it develop based on values like courage, compassion, and justice. How do these values still affect the Jewish nation's identity today?

How Do We Know...

Ancient Iron Age figurine

About Am Yisrael's Early Days?

What do you think is the main source for our ancient history? If you guessed the Bible, you are correct. Although the *Tanakh*, the Jewish Bible, is not a history book, and does not give precise dates or photos, it is where we go to learn much of our earliest history. Whether you believe that all the events in the Tanakh happened or not, its accounts are part of our Jewish heritage and have shaped our people's identity.

Name some events from the history of Am Yisrael that are mentioned in the Tanakh.

In addition to clues from the Tanakh, we use archaeological finds like clothing, jugs, and remains of ancient buildings to help us imagine what life was like in the early days of ancient Israel. Houses and even cities have been discovered from the time of the First Temple. Our knowledge of ancient Jewish history is helped by the discoveries of ancient art and texts that shed light on Bible stories, such as how some famous cities in Israel were conquered. New items are still being found that fill in the gaps in our knowledge of the earliest periods of Jewish history.

About 722 BCE	**586 BCE**	**538–516 BCE**	**About 445 BCE**
Northern kingdom of Israel destroyed by Assyrians	Destruction of the First Temple and exile to Babylonia	Return to Israel and building of the Second Temple	Nehemiah leads the rebuilding of Jerusalem's walls

Taking a Stand

What did it take to be the founding parents of the Jewish nation? In the Tanakh, Abraham is called *Ha'Ivri*, the Hebrew. Literally, this name means "one who came from the other side." This can refer to Abraham's move from his birthplace to Canaan. But it can also refer to the way Abraham and his wife Sarah stood up for beliefs that set them apart from everyone else. While everyone in their time believed in multiple gods and worshipped idols, they introduced **monotheism**, the idea of one God, to the ancient world.

Later, in Egypt, Joseph was called a Hebrew. There, despite the temptations of Egyptian life in the palace, he stayed true to the values of his ancestors. The Jewish community in Egypt continued to be known as Hebrews and held onto its distinct identity instead of adopting the Egyptian religion and culture. Wherever Jews have lived, they learned from their ancestors and continued to pass down their beliefs. Can you describe a time in your life when you took a stand for something you believed in?

From Family to Nation

In the Torah, God promised Abraham that his offspring would be as numerous as the stars in the sky and the grains of sand on the beach. The Torah provides us with a look at the growth of the Jewish people. Number these quotes in order from 1 to 5:

- [ ] "All the people in the house of Jacob who came to Egypt was seventy." (Genesis 46:27)
- [ ] "Moses recorded them in the wilderness of Sinai . . . all the Israelite [men] aged twenty years and over . . . totaled 603,550." (Numbers 1:19, 1:45-46)
- [ ] "Abraham gave the name Isaac to the son he had, to whom Sarah had just given birth." (Genesis 21:3)
- [ ] "[In Egypt] the Israelites were fruitful, and increased greatly, and the land was filled with them." (Exodus 1:7)
- [ ] "[Isaac and Rebecca's son] Jacob had twelve sons." (Genesis 35:22)

The Numbering of the Israelites, **Henri Philippoteaux (1815-1884)**

Do you think God kept his promise to Abraham? Why or why not?

_____

_____

Do you know how many Jewish people there are in the world today? How can you find out?

_____

_____

_____

Leading the Jewish Nation

What are some defining qualities of great Jewish leaders? The Jewish nation has had many leaders who brought them through difficult times in history. Help solve these historical crises by circling the correct answer.

1. Shiphrah and Puah

The powerful Pharaoh commanded the Hebrew midwives in Egypt, Shiphrah and Puah, to kill all the baby boys born to the Israelites. What did they do?

a. Disguised the baby boys as girls.
b. Let the boys live and made up an excuse to explain their actions to Pharaoh.
c. Killed the Jewish baby boys, to save their own lives.

2. Moses

Moses sent spies to check out the land of Canaan. When the spies returned, they reported that the Canaanite people were strong. Many Israelites wanted to return to Egypt rather than enter Canaan. God threatened to destroy the Israelites and start over with Moses. How did Moses respond to God?

a. Thanked God for deciding to spare him at least.
b. Suggested God send the Israelites back to Egypt.
c. Asked God to have compassion for the Israelites and not destroy them.

3. King David

King David knew that his end was near and found out that his son Adonijah had declared himself king. But David had chosen his son Solomon to take over after his death. How did King David react?

a. Immediately crowned Solomon as king.
b. Split the kingdom in half.
c. Sent both sons into exile.

4. Queen Esther

Mordechai warned Queen Esther that all the Jews in the Persian Empire would be destroyed unless she asked King Aḥashverosh to save them. But it was forbidden to visit the king without an invitation and could cost Esther her life. What did Esther do?

a. Refused to help her people.
b. At first held back but then made a plan for approaching the king.
c. Asked her servant to go to King Ahasuerus and risk her life instead.

Answers 1: b, 2: c, 3: a, 4: b

What values or leadership qualities did these leaders demonstrate by their actions?

_____

Which of these leaders do you think had the greatest impact on Jewish history? Why?

_____

Give an example of how these values or leadership qualities could be used to solve a problem in the world today, or in your own life.

_____

From Exile to Exodus

What comes to mind when you hear the word *freedom*? In Jewish history, the idea of freedom is often linked to the Exodus from Egypt, which we celebrate on Passover each year. Freedom meant the end of slavery in Egypt, the opportunity to receive the Torah, and the return of the Israelites to their homeland. The themes of exile and return have since repeated themselves over and over in Jewish history. What does freedom mean to you?

Mapping the Path of the Jewish Nation

The history of the Jewish nation begins in ancient Mesopotamia and Canaan. Canaan, as the Land of Israel was known then, was the Promised Land of the Israelites, and all paths led back to it. But the course of the Jewish nation has not been straight. Plot the travels below by locating each place on the map and drawing an arrow from one place to another. Label each arrow with the number that matches the statement. One example has been filled in for you.

1. Abraham is born in **Mesopotamia**. He and Sarah move to **Canaan**.

2. Joseph is sold and taken from **Canaan** to **Egypt**. Jacob, his children, and their families eventually join him there.

3. The Israelites leave **Egypt** and spend forty years in the **Sinai desert**.

4. Led by Joshua, the Israelites settle in **Canaan**, which is later called Israel.

5. Israel is divided into two kingdoms, **Israel** in the north and **Judah** in the south. The ten tribes of the northern kingdom of **Israel** are exiled to **Assyria**.

6. Jerusalem falls, and the people are exiled from the kingdom of **Judah** to **Babylonia**.

7. Under Persian rule, the Jews return from **Babylonia** to **Israel**, with leaders Ezra and Nehemiah.

In which places did members of the Jewish nation spend time in exile?

_____

Which part of the Jewish nation did *not* return to Israel? _____

How do you think the patterns of exile and return have affected the identity of Am Yisrael?

_____

_____

Staying True to Your Name

The Tanakh recounts how Jacob, on his way home to Israel after many years, found himself locked in a struggle with a stranger one night. When daybreak came, Jacob discovered that he had wrestled with an angel. In recognition, his name was changed to Israel, or *Yisrael*, meaning "one who wrestled with God." Since then, the Jewish people have been called *Am Yisrael* or *B'nei Yisrael*, the Children of Israel.

***Jacob Wrestling with the Angel*,**
Gustave Doré, 1855

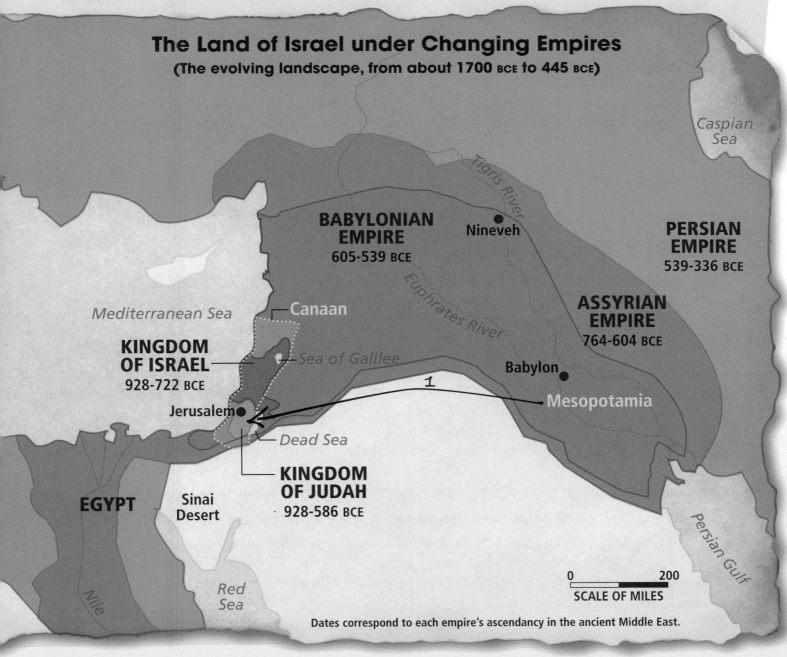

The Land of Israel under Changing Empires
(The evolving landscape, from about 1700 BCE to 445 BCE)

Caspian Sea

BABYLONIAN EMPIRE
605-539 BCE

Nineveh

PERSIAN EMPIRE
539-336 BCE

Tigris River

Mediterranean Sea

Canaan

Euphrates River

ASSYRIAN EMPIRE
764-604 BCE

KINGDOM OF ISRAEL
928-722 BCE

Sea of Galilee

Babylon

Mesopotamia

1

Jerusalem

Dead Sea

KINGDOM OF JUDAH
928-586 BCE

EGYPT

Sinai Desert

Persian Gulf

0   200
SCALE OF MILES

Nile

Red Sea

Dates correspond to each empire's ascendancy in the ancient Middle East.

Then and Now: Jerusalem

Jerusalem has been an important site for the Jewish nation since the times of the Bible.

Then: Ancient Jerusalem

King David conquered Jerusalem and made it the capital of Israel. His son, King Solomon, established the city's importance to Israel when he built what structure there?

_____

Now: Modern Jerusalem

Today, Jerusalem is the capital of the State of Israel, the site of the remains of the Second Temple, and a modern city much larger than the one David and Solomon knew. Can you name a famous building or structure found in Jerusalem today?

_____

Making a Home in Babylonia

The city of Jerusalem was at the heart of Jewish life in ancient Israel. It was the capital city, the place where Israel's royalty lived. Its spiritual and cultural center was the First Temple, built by King Solomon around 950 BCE. But a few centuries later, when the Babylonians conquered the land, things changed. Israel's king and most important officials were taken to Babylonia. Then, in 586 BCE, Jerusalem fell, the Temple was burned to the ground, and the rest of the Jewish nation was sent away from their land. It was a great blow for Am Yisrael. How would they live in exile? How would they keep their Jewish identity and traditions alive without a Temple, a king, or a land of their own?

The prophet Jeremiah sent the Jewish community in Babylonia advice on how to live in exile:

> **Build houses and live in them, plant gardens and eat their fruit. Take wives and have sons and daughters…. Multiply there, do not decrease. And seek the welfare of the city to which I have exiled you and pray to Adonai on its behalf; for in its prosperity, you will prosper.** (Jeremiah 29:5-7)

What advice would you give to the Jewish community in ancient Babylonia, or any Jewish community today, for keeping their Jewish identity strong? _____

_____

Should I Stay or Should I Go?

After seventy years of exile, the Jews in Babylonia, now part of the Persian Empire, were finally allowed to return to the Land of Israel and rebuild their Temple. It wasn't easy, however. The walls of Jerusalem were crumbling, there was drought in the land, and their neighbors made life hard for them. But leaders like Ezra and Nehemiah helped bring Jewish life back to their beloved homeland. Still, many Jews, especially the wealthier ones, remained behind in Babylonia. Why do you think they stayed?

Imagine you are a Babylonian Jew who returns to Jerusalem. Write a postcard to your friends in Babylonia about your new life. Talk about why you returned to the Land of Israel.

What's in a Name?

Did you know that the first person to be called a *Jew* in our sacred texts was Mordechai, in *Megillat Esther*, the Purim story? Mordechai was part of a wave of exiles from Jerusalem to Babylonia. Since they came from the Kingdom of Judah (or Yehuda), these exiles were called *yehudim*, or Jews, in Babylonia. The kingdom had been named for the tribe of Judah, which was descended from Jacob's son Judah.

Talk about It

In the Torah, Abraham is described as a "stranger and a citizen." How can you be both a stranger and a citizen of the place in which you live?

CHAPTER 3

JEWISH LIFE WITH OR WITHOUT THE TEMPLE

6 B.C.E.

When I woke up this morning, my legs still throbbed from yesterday's long, uphill trek. My parents and I had journeyed from our home in Jericho to the Temple Mount in Jerusalem for the Passover pilgrimage.

Because we arrived after sunset, I didn't get my first glimpse of the Temple complex until this morning. When I crawled out of our tent, I gasped; sprawled before me were thousands of colorful tents, and a sea of humanity. I remember my father saying that "countless multitudes from countless cities come, some over land, others over sea, from east and west and north and south for every feast." But I wasn't prepared for the enormity of it all.

A shofar blast woke my father. He leapt up, bolted outside, and dragged me into the crowd. "We'll miss the morning sacrifice if we don't hurry," he said breathlessly. We scrambled up the steps onto a broad, public square, where dozens of shopkeepers hawked their goods, urging us to buy chickens, cattle, birds, or anything we might need for the sacrifice.

Because pilgrimages are notorious for public unrest, my father urged me to stay near him, but I bulled my way through the crowd and climbed up another set of stairs. I stood face to face with the Southern Temple Wall. As I craned my neck to see the towering rows of gleaming, five-ton stones, a scrawny foreigner crashed into me. The sacrificial lamb he was carrying jumped from his arms and scurried away. The man screamed something in a foreign tongue and ran after it.

The day had barely begun, but I knew it would be the greatest day of my life.

Shaul

KEY EVENTS

About 332 BCE	About 167 BCE	About 142 BCE	About 4 BCE
The Land of Israel becomes part of the Greek Empire	The Maccabean Revolt begins	The Jewish state in Israel wins its independence under the Hasmoneans	Birth of Jesus

The Center of Jewish Life

What do you think is the center of Jewish life in your community? Is it a synagogue, where everyone gathers to pray and read the Torah on Shabbat and holidays? Is it your religious school or a Jewish community center? In the time of the Second Temple, Jews lived in towns across Israel and in the Diaspora, but they still considered Jerusalem to be the center of Jewish life. Many traveled to the Holy Temple in Jerusalem for holidays, and the *kohanim*, priests, offered up animal sacrifices for the whole nation there. Jewish rulers and the highest court were based in Jerusalem, too, so the religious laws developed in the capital affected Jews all over Israel and beyond. The Temple was a source of pride for Am Yisrael and kept the Jewish people united.

How Do We Know...

Model of the Second Temple, in Jerusalem

About the Second Temple?

For an insider's view of what life in the Temple was like, the Mishnah and Talmud, our sacred books of Jewish law, are useful. The Mishnah was begun during the time of the Second Temple, and its laws give a glimpse of what went on there. The Talmud gives us detailed descriptions of what it was like to celebrate holidays in the Temple, as well as accounts of what happened there on regular days. We also have books written by the famous Jewish historian Josephus Flavius, who lived through the destruction of the Second Temple. If you visit Jerusalem, you can see the remains of buildings from the Second Temple complex and an ancient road traveled by pilgrims as they made their way to the Temple. Can you name the most famous remnant of the Second Temple?

_____

66 CE	**70 CE**	**About 200 CE**	**About 500 CE**
The Great Revolt against the Romans begins	The Romans destroy the Second Temple and take Jews into exile	The Mishnah is compiled	The Babylonian Talmud is compiled

Lighting the Way

Did you know that the triumph we celebrate on the holiday of Ḥanukkah was not a complete victory? We light the Ḥanukkah menorah to recall how the Maccabees took back control of the Temple, but there were still many battles to go before they would win independence in Israel. So why does Ḥanukkah celebrate this moment? For the Maccabees, religious freedom was the most important victory, and having the Temple in Jewish hands again meant this was possible.

The Second Temple and Jerusalem were the focus of many struggles in the history of the Jewish nation. After Jews returned to Israel from the Babylonian exile, they had to learn how to live in a land that was also part of a larger empire, with limited power to rule themselves. To make matters more complicated, Jews fought among themselves over how to deal with the ruling powers, how to define the Jewish religion, and even how to run the Temple. But despite everything, this time period saw the creation of traditions in Judaism that would light the way for Am Yisrael for centuries to come, even without the Temple.

Queen Salome Alexandra: Keeping the Peace

Maintaining peace with foreign powers, solving conflicts between different Jewish groups, and even keeping things calm between competitive sons—this was the life of Queen Salome Alexandra. Being the last ruler of the independent Jewish state, Judea, was no easy job, but Queen Salome Alexandra pulled it off. She brought peace and prosperity to the land, in the first century BCE, and she invited the Pharisees to be part of her government. This was in stark contrast to the previous ruler, her husband, Alexander Yannai, who was cruel to the sages and even had some of them killed.

Write a question that you would like to ask Queen Salome Alexandra about her life or times:

_____

_____

_____

Josephus: Traitor or Hero?

The Jewish historian Josephus was a commander of the Jewish forces in northern Israel during the Great Revolt against Rome in the first century CE. When the Romans invaded, he surrendered to them, instead of committing suicide with the other Jewish fighters, as they had agreed. He was taken prisoner and then freed and brought to Rome. There he took the Roman name Josephus Flavius, and became a Roman citizen and advisor to the emperor. He wrote books about Jewish history, including the revolt against Roman occupation. Josephus's books are one of the few sources we have for Jewish history in this time period, but he wrote them for the winners of the revolt, the Romans, so historians today don't fully trust his accuracy.

Do you think Josephus was a traitor for surrendering? Or a hero for preserving Jewish history?

_____

_____

Taking Sides

Jews hotly debated many issues during Second Temple times. Read about some burning issues and the views of major groups about them. Decide which side makes more sense to you and explain why.

Side 1	The Issue	Side 2

Maccabees
The Hasmonean family

We've had enough. We want our religious freedom and our Temple back. Jewish law should rule in the Land of Israel, not Greek customs. Let's fight Antiochus!

In 168 BCE, Antiochus, the king of the Syrian-Greek Empire, turns the Temple into a pagan house of worship and decrees that Jews cannot keep their religion.

How should the Jews react?

Hellenizers
Jews who embraced Greek culture

Greek culture has so much to offer, with its great philosophers and beautiful art. Let's embrace their customs, not fight them.

I agree with _____

Sadducees
Jewish priests and upper class

We don't need the Oral Law to help us interpret the Torah. If anyone is to make interpretations, it should be our priests who run the Temple.

Generations of sages created the Oral Law, explanations and commentaries on the Torah.

Should Jews follow this Oral Law, or should we only follow the Torah?

Pharisees
Scribes and sages

Both the Written Law and the Oral Law were given to Moses at Mount Sinai. We need the Oral Law to help us understand the Written Law.

I agree with _____

Sages
Moderate Jewish leaders

The Roman armies are too powerful. If we surrender, we can find a way to preserve the Torah while living under Roman rule.

The year is 70 CE and Jerusalem is under siege, surrounded by the Romans.

Should the Jews surrender?

Zealots
Jewish rebels against Roman rule

We will not let Rome take over our capital city and continue choosing our leaders. We will fight to regain our glory in our own land.

I agree with _____

In some cases, when Jews fought back they won their battles, as the Maccabees did. At other times, they lost the fight, as the Zealots did. But at the same time, they found a way for Judaism and the Jewish nation to survive. Can you think of a great debate among Jews today? _____

_____

Living without a Temple

In the year 70 CE, the Great Revolt failed. Jerusalem was conquered by the Romans, the Temple was destroyed, and the Jewish people were sent into exile. There would not be a Jewish state in Israel again for nearly 1,900 years. What was the key to the survival of Am Yisrael in its darkest times? How would the Jewish people pass down their teachings and traditions?

The famous sage Rabbi Akiva had an answer. When the Romans banned the study of Torah after the destruction of the Temple, he continued to teach it, despite the danger. He explained his reasons with a parable:

There was once a fox who tried to outwit the fish in a local river. Seeing the fish fleeing the fishermen's nets, the fox said, "Why don't you come out onto dry land? We'll live together." Recognizing the fox's wily plan, the fish replied that there may be danger in the river, but on the land they would surely die. (Talmud, *Berachot* 61b)

Like a fish that needs water to survive, the Jewish nation held onto its Torah when all else was lost, using its stories, teachings, and commandments to rebuild Jewish life after the great loss of the Temple. In the Land of Israel and in the Diaspora, Torah study and Jewish community became more important than ever.

Then and Now: The Shekel

The shekel coin was first mentioned in the Torah, when Abraham purchased land for "four hundred shekels of silver." (Genesis 23:16)

Then: Second Temple Period

During the Great Revolt against Rome, Jews minted their own coins. This silver shekel has the words "Holy Jerusalem" and a picture of a Jewish symbol, a red fruit with many seeds. Can you identify the symbol?

_____

Now: Modern Israel

Today, the currency of the modern State of Israel is the New Israeli Shekel. Images on the coins help keep Jewish history alive. Why do you think a lyre is shown on the back of this half-shekel coin?

_____

Creating Community: Synagogues and Schools

After the Temple was gone, Jewish life in ancient Israel, in Babylonia, and elsewhere began to focus more on the local community, including synagogues and Jewish schools. In the synagogue, the main activities were prayer services and the public reading of the Torah. In schools, boys learned to read the Tanakh so that they would be prepared to read the Torah portion and *Haftarah* in synagogue. When they got older, some students continued at another school where they studied the Oral Law. In Babylonia, sages studied the Oral Law in huge academies, and their discussions eventually became part of the Talmud.

Uncovering Synagogue Secrets

Some of the oldest synagogues in the world have been discovered in Israel and even in Syria, Turkey, and Italy. The archaeological remains of these synagogues show us that Jews in the ancient world made sure to build synagogues wherever they lived.

The synagogue at Beit Alfa, a town in Israel, was discovered in 1929 and dates to late Talmudic times. We can learn about Jewish life at the time from artifacts such as this synagogue's mosaic floor.

What Jewish symbols can you find in the mosaic? _____

_____

Why do you think these items were included in the synagogue floor? _____

_____

Talk about It

Archaeology is the study of ancient remains. Israeli archaeologist Pesach Bar-Adon called it a "clasping of hands across the centuries." What do you think he meant by this?

Your Turn

Look closely at the Torah Ark in your own synagogue, and at pictures of other Torah Arks. Then design your own Torah Ark. Write a caption for your picture, describing how it is both similar to and different from others.

CHAPTER 4

CREATING JEWISH COMMUNITY:
FROM EAST TO WEST

910 CE

Each week, I watch my father write a letter to my Uncle Shmuel in Rome. Although he left our home in Alexandria more than ten years ago to "ride the sea with merchants on oars and wind," as he put it, I think of him daily. I remember him saying that "sea trade is one of three things that are engaged in by all who live dangerously and are high minded." Everyone says that I inherited his sense of adventure. I hope so.

My father, on the other hand, is bookish and frail for his age. But I've learned never to underestimate him. He started his career as a tanner on the outskirts of Fez, making leather for waterskins and harnesses. His father taught him that foul, smelly trade, which many Muslims said is fit only for infidels, nonbelievers in their faith. He spent his days beating dried animal skins to remove pieces of flesh, and then soaking them to get rid of any hair. At night, however, he studied our holy Torah. Today, he is a respected scholar, speaks five languages, and writes poetry in Arabic.

Whenever I pleaded with my father to send me to Rome as an apprentice to Uncle Shmuel, he cautioned me, "We are a protected people throughout the caliphate because of our knowledge of the Torah. Master it first, and then make your way in the world."

I'm not sure I've mastered our sacred texts, but today, finally, I depart on my first sea voyage, to join my uncle as he trades in textiles and spices. The chaos of the port fills me with joy. My father hands me a letter for my uncle, and I tuck it safely away in my money pouch. I kiss him good-bye, and climb aboard.

Ya'qub

KEY EVENTS

About 300 CE	About 570	About 638	About 950
Roman Empire adopts Christianity as its official religion	Muhammad, founder of Islam, is born	Islam spreads and Jerusalem falls under Muslim control	Golden Age of Spain begins, a time of peace for Jews

A Taste of the World

From sweet challah with raisins, to the light spongy Ethiopian *injera* bread, to the Middle Eastern pita with its hollow center, breaking bread in the global Jewish community brings tasty surprises. The incredible diversity in Jewish customs today, from our holiday traditions to our cuisine and even our names, is a result of the Jewish Diaspora, or dispersion around the world.

After the fall of the Second Temple, Jews started communities throughout the Roman Empire, in lands that we know today as Italy, Greece, Turkey, and Egypt. They still looked to the sages in Babylonia and the Land of Israel, which was renamed Palestine, for guidance on Jewish law. As Jews moved farther and farther across the globe, this network of Jewish communities helped them be successful in international trade. In return, Jewish traders helped keep Jewish identity strong by passing along innovations in Jewish life from one community to another.

Meanwhile, great shifts in the world presented Jews with a whole new set of challenges. One major development was the rise of two monotheistic religions, Christianity and Islam, both of which had roots in Judaism. The Roman Empire adopted Christianity around 300 CE, and the Muslim Empire conquered much of the Middle East in the seventh century. As a result, Jews in each area found themselves subject to new kinds of rulers, who granted them different amounts of freedom.

How Do We Know...

About Medieval Jewish Communities?

Even without planes and trains, Jews traveled across the world in medieval times. Most Jewish travelers were traders; others were pilgrims to Jerusalem, scholars, or scribes. Their letters and accounts tell us about Jewish communities and customs. The most famous Jewish traveler was Benjamin of Tudela. His journeys in the twelfth century took him from Spain through Europe and into Israel, to Africa, and even as far eastward as India. Fascinated by what he saw, he wrote about the different synagogues he visited and what Jews did for a living, and he gave us a window into their everyday lives. We also learn about medieval Jewish life from the many letters Jews wrote to rabbis, sometimes halfway across the world, about questions of Jewish law. In addition, beautifully illustrated manuscripts survive that show scenes of Jewish life.

This portrait, *Susskind, the Jew of Trimberg,* depicts a thirteenth-century German Jewish poet.

About 1070	1096	1099	1180
Rashi establishes a yeshiva in Troyes, France	The First Crusade begins, setting off attacks on Jews in France and Germany	Crusaders conquer Jerusalem	Maimonides completes the *Mishneh Torah*, his code of Jewish law

In the East: Jews in the Muslim Empire

"In Baghdad there are about forty thousand Jews and they dwell in security, prosperity, and honor under the great caliph, and among them are great sages, the heads of academies engaged in the study of the law." —Benjamin of Tudela

Pages from the Koran, the Muslim holy book

Benjamin of Tudela's words give us a glimpse into one of the largest medieval Jewish communities, Baghdad, which flourished under Muslim rule. Like Jews, Muslims, the followers of Islam, believe in monotheism and in many of the Jewish prophets. But Muslims believe that Muhammad was the final prophet, and they follow his teachings.

Muslim leaders conquered lands stretching from modern-day Afghanistan, through Iran and Iraq, and westward as far as Spain. Like Christians, Jews who came under Muslim rule were given a special status, called *dhimmis*, or "People of the Book." They were a protected minority and were allowed to practice their religion, but they were not considered equal. Laws forbade Jews from building synagogues that were higher than mosques. Unlike Muslims, Jews could not carry weapons to protect themselves, and they had to pay special taxes. Why do you think Jews were given a special status?

Solomon Schechter

A Time Capsule of Medieval Jewish Life

Imagine if you kept all your used school notebooks, old quizzes, drawings, and birthday cards—for years and years. Eventually, it would be a time capsule of your life. Something similar happened in the attic of the Ben Ezra Synagogue in the old city of Cairo. All kinds of documents were kept in a *genizah*, a place where holy Hebrew-language documents are deposited when they are no longer needed or in usable condition. In this case, everyday items that had Hebrew letters were also included. This went on for centuries. In the late 1800s, this time capsule came to the attention of Solomon Schechter, a rabbi and scholar. As he pulled out dusty pages from old *haggadot* and fragments of letters from long ago, he realized he had his hands on a treasure trove of information about medieval Jewish life.

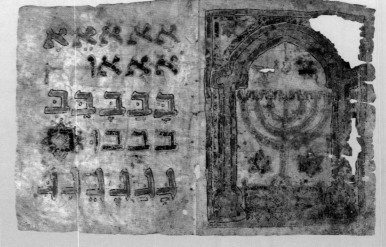

Page from a tenth-century Hebrew primer, found in the Cairo Genizah

The Secrets of the Genizah

Kids' doodles, colorful *k'tubot* (wedding contracts), a letter from Maimonides, poems, business receipts of spice traders, a Bible written in Arabic…the hundreds of items in the Cairo Genizah create a picture of Jewish life in medieval times. Fill in the sentences below using the word bank.

Did you know that in the medieval Islamic world…

… Jews wrote and spoke _____ and _____ .

… Jewish men were _____ and _____ .

… Jewish women could be _____ .

… Jews traded in _____ , _____ , and _____ .

… there were Jewish communities in _____ , _____ , and _____ .

> **Word Bank:** Iraq, traders, gems, Yemen, Arabic, teachers, Persian, exotic spices, doctors, Spain, silks

I Am My Brother's Keeper

For many reasons, life for Jews was uncertain during medieval times. Restrictive laws, dangers involved in travel and trading, and changing relationships with non-Jewish neighbors meant that Jews had to look out for each other. A letter from the Cairo Genizah shows how Maimonides, the famous Torah scholar, philosopher, and physician, raised funds to help redeem captives, an urgent mitzvah because Jews were often kidnapped.

"Dear brothers, pay attention. . . . Act as we have done, we the judges, elders, and scholars. We all go around day and night and solicit the people, in the synagogues, in the bazaar, and at the gates of their houses . . . and this after we ourselves have contributed as much as we have been able to do. Likewise, you will act on behalf of the captives." —Maimonides

Why does Maimonides urge Jews to give tzedakah to help Jews in other communities?

_____

_____

How does your community raise support for a cause?

_____

_____

Your Turn

Create a time capsule for your Jewish community. What items would you add to show people of the future how your community celebrated Jewish holidays, taught its children the Torah, or helped its neediest members?

Think about what items you will choose, how you will get them, and what you will place them in.

מא כרב מימון

Signature of Maimonides

In the West: Jews in Christian Lands

Like Jews in the Muslim Empire, Jews in Germany and France also were allowed to govern their own community, called the **kehillah**. Their world also was influenced by an official state religion, this time Christianity. Christianity is rooted in the stories of the Jewish Bible, which Christians call the Old Testament. But the Christian Bible also includes the New Testament, which teaches about Jesus, who Christians believe was the son of God.

Armies of the First Crusade

Christians in the Middle Ages viewed Jews with great suspicion. They accused the Jewish people of rejecting the truths brought by Christianity to the world and even of causing Jesus's death. The result was that Christian society limited the amount of contact that Jews could have with Christians. The Jewish community instead focused on its internal life and kept mostly separate from Christian neighbors. As Christian persecution rose, the situation for Ashkenazi Jews became increasingly less secure. During the First Crusade in 1096, many Jewish communities in Germany were destroyed. More attacks followed, and eventually Jews were forced to leave and find homes in safer lands.

Centered on the Torah

Jews first came to Europe for trading opportunities, but by the eleventh century, large families headed by Torah scholars had settled in European cities and brought with them a passion for Torah and Talmud study. Rashi, the well-known Torah scholar and commentator, and his descendants had a major impact on how the Torah and Talmud were studied and taught. The way we learn Torah today is based on the hard work of these scholars, who built great *yeshivot* (schools), wrote the first commentaries, and emphasized the importance of Torah study for the survival of the Jewish nation.

Words to Know: Ashkenazic

Your family's names, traditional recipes, and even seder customs all give clues to your family's roots. Many Jewish families in America emigrated from Europe and brought a unique way of Jewish life with them, an **Ashkenazic** lifestyle. In medieval days, Germany was called *Ashkenaz* in Hebrew, and so the Jews of Germany and neighboring France became known as *Ashkenazim*. These Jewish communities later brought their traditions with them to Poland and other countries, and continue to have an impact on the American Jewish community even today.

Talk about It

What do you think helped Jews in medieval times keep their Jewish identity strong?

Life in the Community

Compare Jewish life in medieval Ashkenazic communities to your own community.

Feature	Medieval Ashkenazic community	My own community (Fill in descriptions below)
Passover seder	Your seder would include four cups of red wine; small, round, handmade *matzot;* a handwritten haggadah; and *ḥaroset* made from nuts, apples, spices, and wine.	
Legal system	If you have a dispute with a neighbor, you might go to the *beit din*, a rabbinical court, for a resolution by its rabbis.	
Synagogue worship	If you are a girl, you might pray with your mother in the synagogue, helped by a female prayer leader. If you are a boy, you learn how to lead prayers and read the Torah, and you attend synagogue with your father.	
Role of the rabbi	Your rabbi spends most of his time giving lectures, answering questions of Jewish law, teaching Torah, and serving on a *beit din*.	
School	If you are a boy, you begin *ḥeder*, a Jewish elementary school, at age five or six, where you study Hebrew, the Torah, and prayers. If you are a girl, you learn at home, studying *mitzvot*, Bible stories, and some Hebrew. Both boys and girls might also learn basic reading, writing, and math.	
Higher education	Your city might have a *yeshiva*, a Jewish school for older boys, that specializes in Talmudic study. Students often return home to become leaders in their own communities.	

If you were to travel back in time to a Jewish community in medieval Europe, what might seem most familiar to you? What might be most different?

_____

_____

_____

_____

_____

_____

The Role of the Rabbi

Did you know that Jewish leaders and Torah scholars were originally called "rabbis" in the Mishnah? The sages used it as a sign of honor, since it means "my master" and is based on the Hebrew word for "great one." Today, a rabbi still has to study a lot before earning that title, but a rabbi's job requires many other skills as well. What skills do you think a rabbi needs?

CHAPTER 5

CROSSING CONTINENTS, STARTING OVER

Spain, 1415

Dear Diary,

This is my first journal entry as a converso, a New Christian. How strange it feels to write these words, and how strange it feels to live as something other than a Jew. From today onward, therefore, I must live like Queen Esther. When she entered Ahashverosh's palace, she concealed her identity but stayed true to the God of Israel. I too will act as a non-Jew on the outside but remain a hidden Jew on the inside.

My parents chose this fate for our family last year, when the religious debates in Tortosa finally ended. From the minute the Christian pope ordered our rabbis to stand before him and defend our holy texts, I feared the worst. The debates enflamed the community, and the authorities took severe actions against us. Some, including my aunt and uncle, escaped and have wandered afar to the ends of the world. But my parents could not afford the high prices demanded by the ship captains, so we stayed and were baptized.

At first, life was easier, but soon no one trusted us. Not only did the Christians doubt that our conversion was sincere, but also our brethren who had stayed true to their faith and didn't convert doubted our hidden loyalty. I feel trapped and hated by everyone. There is only endless suffering if I remain, so tomorrow, I will start making a plan to flee. Portugal? Eretz Yisrael? I know not, but I will trust in the God of Israel to guide me.

Maria (Malka)

KEY EVENTS

1306 and 1394	1453	1475	1492
Jews are expelled from France	Ottoman Empire gains control of Constantinople, and welcomes Jews	Rashi's commentary on the Torah is the first printed Hebrew-language book	Christopher Columbus arrives in the New World

On the Move

Today, if you visit a synagogue in another city or town, you may find tunes and customs that come from all over the world. As Jewish communities became more independent from the original centers of Jewish life in Israel and Babylonia, they developed their own unique Jewish character. By the end of the fifteenth century, Jews not only lived in the Middle East and its neighboring areas, but had spread out across the continent of Europe.

European Jews benefited from new advances in technology, like the invention of the printing press, and flourished in all kinds of new businesses. But they were often caught between warring powers or local rulers and jealous citizens or peasants, making life difficult and often dangerous. When European expansion and exploration offered the promise of greater freedoms, Jews took the opportunity to put down roots in new places, even crossing continents. The Jewish map was changing and expanding, setting the stage for the Jewish world we know today.

Spotlight On...

Jewish Girls and Women

What was life like for Jewish girls and women during this time? Unfortunately, most Jewish women did not write about their lives, and what they may have written has been lost to history. We do know that they were taught how to manage a household, a demanding job that included cooking over an open fire, making clothing, and raising children. Girls received a basic education at home that included a foundation in the Torah, knowledge needed to lead a Jewish life.

From the *Rothschild Miscellany*, fifteenth-century Italy

Many Jewish women worked outside the home, too, although their opportunities varied depending on where they lived. There were Jewish women moneylenders in medieval Europe, doctors and businesswomen in both medieval Europe and Egypt, and printers and editors in fifteenth- and sixteenth-century Italy. Women did not hold public roles, like being a rabbi or judge on a Jewish court, but they did their part to maintain and pass on Jewish tradition at home. Some educated women, like the daughters of the great Torah scholar Rashi, taught Jewish law to women in the community, while others led women in prayer in the synagogue.

1492	1516	1565	1654
Jews are expelled from Spain	In Italy, the first ghetto is established, a specific area in which Jews must live	Publication of the *Shulḥan Aruch* by Rabbi Joseph Karo	The first Jews arrive in New Amsterdam, now New York

The Jews of Spain: From the Golden Age to an Era of Persecution

Replica of Columbus's ship, *La Pinta*

The Jews of Spain flourished under Muslim rule for centuries. Encouraged and influenced by the surrounding Islamic culture, they made important contributions to the sciences, literature, and the arts. During this Golden Age, Jews also created their own brand of Jewish music, philosophy, poetry, and even cuisine. Unfortunately, this peaceful period came to an end when Christian powers took back control of Spain in the eleventh century. There was a lot of pressure for Jews in Spain to convert to Christianity, and as a result, many Jews became New Christians, or **conversos**. Some, called crypto-Jews, kept their Jewish traditions in secret. Many conversos were arrested, tortured, and killed by the Spanish Inquisition, an institution established by the Spanish king and queen in 1480, aimed at determining whether converts were true Christians or not.

A Community Uprooted

When you hear the date 1492, what jumps to mind? You might say it is the year that Christopher Columbus arrived in the New World. But did you know that it is also a date associated with a terrible tragedy for the Jewish people? Christians worried that the large Jewish community in Spain was helping conversos stay connected to their Judaism, and so in 1492 the country's rulers forced all the Jews of Spain to leave.

This event, called the Spanish Expulsion, had lasting effects on the Jewish nation, who mourned the destruction of the vibrant Spanish Jewish community. Some of the conversos who stayed in Spain did their best to maintain an underground version of Judaism. But **Sephardic** Jewish life in Spain was destroyed. The tens of thousands of Jews expelled from Spain fanned out across the world, creating the Sephardic Diaspora. However, Columbus's explorations opened up a new world for Europeans, and a new beginning for many Jews. In fact, the first Jews in North America were of Spanish-Portuguese descent.

Words to Know: Sephardic

Just as Ashkenazic Jews came from one region in Europe and brought their unique Jewish traditions with them across the world, so did the Sephardic Jews of Spain. The Hebrew word for Spain is *Sepharad*, and so Jews from Spain and nearby Portugal became known as Sephardim. If your family's ancestors came from Spain or Portugal, you may have Sephardic customs or foods that are different from Ashkenazic ones. Can you think of any examples?

Buñuelos, a popular Sephardic Ḥanukkah treat

As One Door Closes, Another Opens

Sephardic Jews found new homes and had an impact on each place they moved, changing the character of many Jewish communities and contributing valuable knowledge and skills. Unscramble the words to find the names of cities in which they made their mark.

_____ ESFDA: Jewish learning, mysticism, and poetry

_____ TARSDMMAE: Trade networks and business skills

_____ SBINLUAT: Knowledge of printing

_____ _____ ENW ESMATMRDA: A fight for freedom of religion

_____ EFIRCE: The developing sugar industry

_____ NOONDL: Banking skills

_____ NVEIEC: Music, the arts, cooking traditions

Most of these cities are ports, located beside rivers or oceans. Why do you think that Sephardic Jews were especially welcomed in port cities?

_____

_____

_____

Doña Gracia: The Angel of the Marranos

Called "the Angel of the Marranos [conversos]," or simply *La Senora* (the Lady), Doña Gracia Mendes Nasi dedicated herself to helping other Jews. Born into a converso family in Portugal in about 1510, she knew firsthand about their hardships, and once free, she did everything she could to help other conversos escape the Inquisition in Portugal and start new lives in safer countries. She helped them learn about their religion by funding Spanish translations of Hebrew books. In Istanbul, she helped build Jewish schools, hospitals, and synagogues; and she worked to establish a community in Tiberias, in the Land of Israel, so Jews would have a safe place to settle.

Jews of Ashkenaz: Starting Over

Crusader's shield

Life for Ashkenazi Jews in Europe was also uncertain. During the Middle Ages, Christians were increasingly suspicious of Jews, even blaming them for devastating plagues and accusing them of terrible crimes. Christian rulers put distance between themselves and Jewish communities by limiting Jews to very few jobs, such as money lending. This made it hard for Jews to earn a living and further damaged relations with Christians, who resented owing Jews money. Starting with the Crusades, violence against Jews increased. From the 1300s through the 1500s, several European countries expelled their Jewish residents, and so the Jews of France, Germany, and England searched for new places to live.

Many Ashkenazi Jews streamed into Poland, which welcomed Jews as the country expanded. There, Jews were granted greater religious freedoms and legal rights. Polish Jews were merchants, minted coins, managed salt mines, and even ran the estates of Polish noblemen. By the sixteenth century, Poland was a center for Jewish study and Ashkenazi life, and it would remain that way for several centuries.

Building a New Jewish Community

In Poland, Ashkenazi Jews were allowed to rule their own communities through an institution called the Council of the Four Lands. Jews established their own schools, courts, and synagogues in each town, as they had in their previous homes, and imported their language, Yiddish, a mixture of Hebrew and German.

Imagine that you are part of a group of ten Jewish families who must move to a place where there are no Jews. How will you build a new Jewish community? Choose the three institutions that you would build first, from the word bank, and explain why they are important.

Word Bank:
Beit din (Jewish court)
Hebrew/religious school
Jewish cemetery
Jewish community center
Jewish day camp
Jewish museum
Jewish preschool
Jewish youth group
Kosher butcher
Kosher restaurant
Synagogue

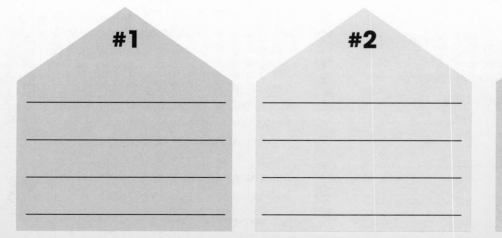

#1

#2

#3

Jewish Traditions Jeopardy

If you were a guest at a Jewish event a few hundred years ago, you might recognize some traditions that are still kept today. Fill in a question for each answer about a Jewish custom.

Ashkenazic wedding ḥupah

1. At a Passover seder in the fifteenth or sixteenth century, Jewish families used *this* book, most likely handwritten and decorated with beautiful paintings.

   What is a _____ ?

2. By the sixteenth century, it was common for boys turning thirteen in Ashkenazic communities to read the Torah as part of *this* life-cycle event.

   What is a _____ ?

3. After lighting the *ḥanukkiyah*, many Ashkenazic families played *this*, based on a German children's game.

   What is a _____ ?

4. By the 1500s, Ashkenazic Jewish brides and grooms often got married under *this* item.

   What is a _____ ?

5. Possibly inspired by local carnivals, Italian Jews are believed to be the first Jews to have worn *this* holiday item.

   What is a _____ ?

Word Bank:
bar mitzvah, dreidel, haggadah, ḥupah, Purim costume

Talk about It

Do you know if your family's origins are Sephardic or Ashkenazic? How can you find out? What do you think it would be like if you had to hide your Jewish identity, as the crypto-Jews did?

Glückel of Hameln: Portrait of an Ashkenazic Life

A highly respected Jewish businesswoman, Glückel of Hameln wrote a lively account of her life in seventeenth-century Germany, giving us a valuable glimpse of Ashkenazic life at the time. How do you think her description of her daughter's lavish wedding compares to a modern Jewish wedding?

We sailed from Altona…. Fourteen days before the marriage we set forth with timbrels and with dances…. As the bridal pair were led beneath the ḥupah out it came that in the confusion we had forgotten to write the wedding contract! What was to be done?… Rabbi Meir declared that the groom should appoint a bondsman to write out the contract immediately after the wedding. Then the rabbi read a set-contract from a book. And so the couple were joined…. After the ceremony, all the distinguished guests were ushered into [the] enormous salon…. There stood the mighty table laden with dainties fit for a king…. When the guests of honor had eaten of the fruit and cakes and had done justice to the wine, the table was cleared…. Then appeared masked performers who…played all manner of entertaining pranks. They concluded…with a truly splendid "Dance of Death."…

And the wedding was brought to a happy end.

CHAPTER 6

WINDS OF CHANGE: NEW OPPORTUNITIES AND RESPONSES

Monday, November 7, 1881

Although my feet are now anchored safely on dry land, my bones still feel the anger of the stormy Atlantic.

My parents and I fled our home in Yelisavetgrad, in the Ukraine, last April, after the pogrom. Because Papa is a skilled tailor and had saved some money, we secured passage to America on a ship called the British Prince. Its name made me think of a luxurious, stately vessel, but how wrong I was! Before our voyage, it had been a cattle ship. We slept beneath the main deck, on narrow, wooden bunks, in a dark, filthy compartment where the cattle once stood.

When we arrived in America, we were taken to Castle Garden, an immigrant depot in New York. Inspectors examined us to make sure we were healthy. Afterwards, we stood in line for five hours to register our names and nationality. A rude clerk snarled something at Papa. To my surprise, he smiled meekly and said nothing. We've slept outside for the past two nights with hundreds of other immigrants. None of us have bathed for more than two weeks, so the stench is terrible, "as if a thousand cats were living here." But the odor doesn't bother me, because I am free, a new American, with a bright and glorious future.

Bluma

KEY EVENTS

1648–1649	1791	1791	1840s
Anti-Jewish violence destroys Jewish communities in Poland	Jews in France achieve emancipation, equal rights	Russia establishes the Pale of Settlement	Wave of Jewish immigration to America from Germany begins

Fighting for Freedom

In America, you and your family are free to live where you want and celebrate your Judaism as you choose. When you are old enough, you will vote for your country's leaders. The promise of this kind of freedom was what drew Colonial Jews to fight for independence alongside American revolutionaries, and later attracted waves of Jewish immigrants from Europe, who helped build the fast-growing United States.

By contrast, most European Jews in the 1600s and 1700s lived in tight-knit Jewish communities that existed almost independently of the larger states of which they were a part. Interaction with their non-Jewish neighbors was minimal, mostly limited to business dealings. In many countries, Jews were only allowed to live in certain areas, such as the Pale of Settlement, a region in Russia. This helped European Jews preserve their traditions and create a strong culture with little outside influence. But many doors were closed to them: they were not allowed to study in most non-Jewish schools and universities, and they could not hold certain jobs, join many social groups and clubs, or take part in politics.

But in the late 1700s and early 1800s the same ideas of equality and freedom that inspired the American Revolution were also causing changes in Europe. A discussion began over how to better include Jews in the state. Jews themselves fought for change. A drive for Jewish equality had begun.

Jewish American Style

Most people in the nineteenth century owned only a few items of clothing, and their choices identified what they did and where they were from. Today we have much more freedom to dress as we like and many styles to choose from. This is in part due to the involvement of American Jews in the clothing industry. Jewish immigrants to America came up with ways to mass-produce clothes so that everyone could afford the latest styles.

One famous example is blue jeans, invented by Jewish tailor Jacob Davis and merchant Levi Strauss. First designed in 1873, these durable pants were originally work wear for cowboys, ranchers, carpenters, and even gold miners. Jeans have since become a hit worldwide, as an expression of personal style.

1881	1885	1887	1896
Pogroms spur mass immigration of Russian Jews to the U.S.	The Reform movement in America calls for a modern approach to Judaism	The Jewish Theological Seminary opens a center for Conservative Jewish studies	Theodor Herzl's book, *The Jewish State*, promotes Zionism

A Changing World for Europe's Jews

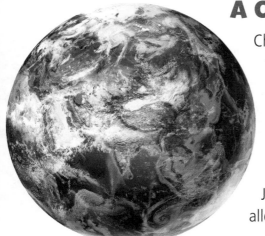

Change was happening in western Europe. European rulers saw that the international trade networks and business skills of their Jewish populations were valuable for their developing economies. Slowly, Jews were allowed back into France, Germany, and England. As Europeans in the eighteenth century spread the ideas of the Enlightenment, a movement based on the values of independent reasoning and freedoms for all, they became more tolerant toward Jews. Western European Jews finally became **emancipated**, allowed to be equal citizens.

Jews eagerly pursued more education, entered new professions, and took part in their country's culture. They found that the Judaism of their parents needed to adapt to a modern world. As they explored a more open society, they were disappointed to still encounter anti-Jewish prejudice, despite the freedoms they were gaining. This sparked new questions for them about their future in Europe.

Meanwhile, in eastern Europe, hardships and pogroms, violent attacks on Jews, continued. Most of the Jews of Russia and Poland still lived in *shtetls*, small towns, living as their parents and grandparents had, with little contact with their non-Jewish neighbors.

Jews across Europe looked for innovative ideas to improve their lives, and took actions that were to make a great difference to their children and grandchildren, including many of your ancestors. This period saw the growth of new movements, including the Reform and Conservative movements, Ḥasidic Judaism, and **Zionism**. Increasing immigration to the United States and Palestine, as the Land of Israel was called then, changed the Jewish map. By the end of the nineteenth century, the Jewish world looked drastically different than ever before, and more similar to the diverse global Jewish community that we live in today.

The Cattle Merchant, by Marc Chagall, 1912

Discussion Board: Debating New Ideas

Imagine that the Internet existed in the 1700s and 1800s. What conversations might have been held online? Respond to each "post" below.

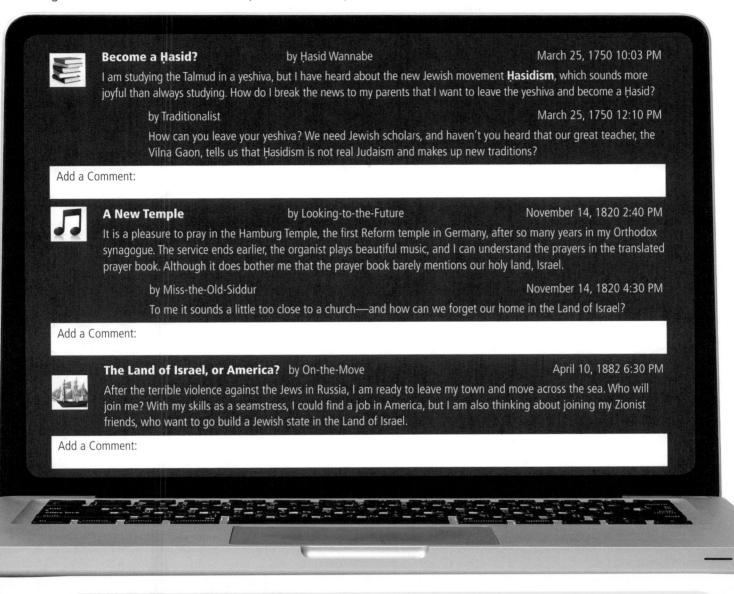

Become a Ḥasid? by Ḥasid Wannabe March 25, 1750 10:03 PM

I am studying the Talmud in a yeshiva, but I have heard about the new Jewish movement **Ḥasidism**, which sounds more joyful than always studying. How do I break the news to my parents that I want to leave the yeshiva and become a Ḥasid?

by Traditionalist March 25, 1750 12:10 PM

How can you leave your yeshiva? We need Jewish scholars, and haven't you heard that our great teacher, the Vilna Gaon, tells us that Ḥasidism is not real Judaism and makes up new traditions?

Add a Comment:

A New Temple by Looking-to-the-Future November 14, 1820 2:40 PM

It is a pleasure to pray in the Hamburg Temple, the first Reform temple in Germany, after so many years in my Orthodox synagogue. The service ends earlier, the organist plays beautiful music, and I can understand the prayers in the translated prayer book. Although it does bother me that the prayer book barely mentions our holy land, Israel.

by Miss-the-Old-Siddur November 14, 1820 4:30 PM

To me it sounds a little too close to a church—and how can we forget our home in the Land of Israel?

Add a Comment:

The Land of Israel, or America? by On-the-Move April 10, 1882 6:30 PM

After the terrible violence against the Jews in Russia, I am ready to leave my town and move across the sea. Who will join me? With my skills as a seamstress, I could find a job in America, but I am also thinking about joining my Zionist friends, who want to go build a Jewish state in the Land of Israel.

Add a Comment:

Coming Together for a Common Cause

In the late nineteenth century, rising **anti-Semitism**, prejudice against Jews, led Jews to consider a dramatic idea—creating a Jewish state in their ancient homeland, Israel. Leaders of this movement, called Zionism, debated how to achieve this goal and what the modern Jewish state should look like. Theodor Herzl, the "Father of Zionism," organized the First Zionist Congress, a big, noisy meeting in 1897 in Basel, Switzerland. There, over two hundred Jews from across the world met for the first time to plan how to turn their vision for a Jewish state into a reality.

Herzl famously said, "If you will it, it is no dream." What do you think he meant? _____

_____

Making It in America

As peddlers, furriers, tailors, rabbis, bankers, and even cowboys, Jewish immigrants settled across America and helped their country grow. The first American Jews were of Spanish-Portuguese descent, and brought Sephardic traditions. Starting in the 1840s, a wave of German Jews arrived, many of whom began as peddlers and went on to run shops, factories, and department stores. When violence threatened Jewish life in Russia in the 1880s, about two million eastern European Jews streamed into America. Jewish immigrants from Poland and Russia brought Yiddish words, such as *oy, nosh, chutzpah,* and *schlep,* words that have made it into the American vocabulary. They also brought ideas, skills, and traditions from the old country, and by the beginning of the twentieth century, the American Jewish community looked very different due to their influence.

The opportunities for immigrants to **assimilate** or fit into American life inspired the famous metaphor of America as a "melting pot" of cultures. How is America like a melting pot?

_____

_____

Today, many people compare American culture to a mosaic or salad bowl instead, in which each element contributes to the whole but keeps its own identity. What metaphor would you use to describe how Jews fit into American life today? Why?

_____

_____

_____

_____

Talk about It

What challenges do you think Jewish immigrants to America have faced?

Your Turn

Create a visual metaphor—a piece of art based on an idea or object you think best represents Jews in American life today. It could be a melting pot, mosaic, salad bowl, or something else. Consider making a photo collage, a paper sculpture, or a collage of different materials and recycled objects.

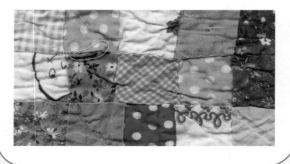

Hebrew
עִבְרִית

Kosher
food

I Went to America and I Took with Me...

Jewish immigrants to America brought with them ritual objects, traditions, and even values from their home countries. However, they often had to choose carefully what to bring when they came to America. They had limited room to pack, and not everything would be useful in their new home. What would you choose to bring? Choose five items from the trunk that would help preserve your Jewish traditions and values in a new land, and explain your choices.

Jewish Identity Packing List

I would bring…   because…

1. _____   _____

2. _____   _____

3. _____   _____

4. _____   _____

5. _____   _____

Emma Lazarus: Helping the Newest Immigrants

Each wave of Jewish immigration built up the American Jewish community. Those who had already made lives for themselves in America often helped the newest immigrants. So when Emma Lazarus, a Sephardic Jewish poet, saw the poverty and sickness that new Russian Jewish immigrants were experiencing, she got involved and organized aid for them. Their suffering inspired her famous poem "The New Colossus," which is inscribed on the Statue of Liberty's pedestal and whose words read in part:

> Give me your tired, your poor,
> Your huddled masses yearning to breathe free,
> The wretched refuse of your teeming shore.
> Send these, the homeless, tempest-tossed to me,
> I lift my lamp beside the golden door!

What is the main idea of this poem? _____

_____

Describe a time when you have been inspired to help others. What inspired you?

_____

_____

CHAPTER 7

ON THE WORLD'S STAGE

Palestine, 1907

Dearest cousin,

When I left Gomel for Palestine, you pleaded with me to stay in our tiny Russian village, though it had been victimized by violence, yet again. I answered your whimpers with the slogan that now guides my life: "In blood and fire Judea went down, in blood and fire Judea shall rise again." Perhaps these words sounded harsh and uncaring to your ear. If so, I beg for your forgiveness; but I do not regret having spoken them. The Jewish problem will never be solved by a revolution against the Czar. Instead, we must turn our energies toward creating a new life in our ancient homeland.

Like my brothers-in-arms in the military group we call Shomrim, I believe Jews have lived meekly in exile for too long. As a result, our people have forgotten the redeeming value of labor, and the ennobling power of self-defense. Cousin, do not confuse old habits with nature. Tell everyone who will listen that "Jewish boys, lately from the ghettoes of Europe, should handle guns, manage horses, stand up to a fight, and organize a defense." Let my cowardly neighbors in Gomel know that with no more than nineteen members, the Shomrim refuse to cower before the Arab enemy. Our principles are clear: self-defense, not revenge; restraint, patience, and intelligence. What can be done by friendliness should not be done by force. Please, cousin, tarry no longer. Join us, soon!

Meyer

KEY EVENTS

1881–1948	1909	1917	1939–1945
Waves of Jewish immigrants enter Palestine	First kibbitz founded in Palestine	The Russian Revolution overthrows the czar, and Communist rule begins	The Second World War and the Holocaust destroy European Jewish life

Devastation and Triumph

The twentieth century saw great highs and lows for the Jewish people. The fall of old empires in Europe, the Middle East, and Africa, and the rise of newly independent nations offered Jews more opportunities but, in some cases, unleashed forces that made it impossible for them to stay. The anti-Jewish violence that had been developing in the previous century gathered strength and, in its darkest form during World War II, destroyed European Jewish life.

And yet on the heels of that devastation came the Zionist movement's great triumph, when a Jewish state was finally established in the Land of Israel. This began a new chapter in the life of the Jewish nation, one in which Jews had an opportunity to shape their own future. Building the Jewish state was no simple task, but Zionist pioneers and Jews around the world pitched in. Today, you can see the fruits of their efforts, and those of each generation that has followed, as the modern State of Israel continues to evolve and to thrive.

Spotlight On...

Young pioneers picking oranges on a kibbutz in Palestine, 1938

Jewish Youth Movements

As the world changed, young men and women were at the forefront of new movements in Jewish life. Kids played a role too. It had become common for Jewish children to attend state schools and study secular subjects, and as a result they became more educated about the world. But they still encountered prejudice and hardship. Jewish youth movements became popular in Europe in the early twentieth century as a result, because they gave members a way to connect with other Jewish kids and work toward improving life for all Jews.

Zionist youth groups prepared their members for life as pioneers in Palestine. Their members later built *kibbutzim* in Israel. Jewish youth movement members were also involved in Jewish resistance during World War II. A group of mostly young Jews led the dramatic Warsaw Ghetto uprising, in which Jews fought back against Nazi soldiers. Other groups helped Jews make it to Palestine from Europe after the Holocaust. Jewish youth movements were born out of a need for young people to have a say in the future of the Jewish people, and ultimately played an important role in saving and rebuilding Jewish lives.

1943

Warsaw Ghetto uprising against the Nazis

1948

The modern State of Israel is established

1967

Israel wins the Six-Day War

1991

The Soviet Union collapses; Russian Jews immigrate to Israel and U.S.

Darkening Clouds on the Horizon

Jews around the world have suffered from discrimination for centuries. In some places, Jews were given an official lower status or had to wear identifying clothing; they were limited in the types of jobs they could have or where they could live; and they were restricted in their education and lacked political power. In the worst cases, Jews were barred from practicing their religion, expelled from their country, or even lost their lives. Both Jews and non-Jews debated the roots of anti-Jewish prejudice, with many blaming religious intolerance or economic jealousy.

As the world, especially in western Europe, became more secular and Jews became more integrated into society, they were hopeful that the hatred against them would fade away. So it was a great disappointment when new waves of anti-Jewish feeling arose in Europe in the late nineteenth and early twentieth centuries. Especially in Germany, things became increasingly worse for Jews in the 1930s, where anti-Semites blamed Jews for the poor economy, for losing World War I, and for all kinds of problems in society.

Words to Know: Holocaust, Shoah

It is hard to come up with a name for an event that is so terrible it is beyond our understanding. Some call the Nazi's destruction of European Jews the **Holocaust**, which means "completely burnt offering." Others refer to it as the **Shoah**, a Hebrew word meaning "catastrophe."

Jewish Life in Germany Is Shattered

"Nazis Smash, Loot and Burn Jewish Shops and Temples…" began the shocking headline in the *New York Times* on November 11, 1938. Over the course of two days, there was widespread destruction, synagogues were burned, and many Jews across Germany and Austria were brutally arrested. This event, called *Kristallnacht*, "night of broken glass," marked a turning point in the history of Germany's Jews, who had once seen a promising future in modern Germany. Ever since Adolf Hitler came to power in 1933, the Nazi party had increasingly restricted the rights of Jews, and the atmosphere had become more and more anti-Semitic. Many German Jews tried to leave, but many countries, including the United States, strictly limited the number of Jews allowed in. Jews around the world tried to help German Jews escape, but their power was limited. Kristallnacht was a chilling sign of even worse times to come.

A synagogue burns during Kristallnacht in Nazi Germany.

Through Their Eyes

Anne Frank was a Jewish girl from Holland who lived in hiding during World War II. Her diary is famous for its vivid description of what it was like to live under the Nazis.

Saturday, June 20, 1942

After May 1940 the good times were few and far between.... Our freedom was severely restricted by a series of anti-Jewish decrees: Jews were required to wear a yellow star; Jews were required to turn in their bicycles; Jews were forbidden to use street cars; Jews were forbidden to ride in cars, even their own;...Jews were forbidden to be out on the streets between 8 p.m. and 6 a.m.; Jews were forbidden to attend theaters, movies or any other forms of entertainment; Jews were forbidden to use swimming pools, tennis courts, hockey fields or any other athletic fields.... Jews were forbidden to visit Christians in their homes; Jews were required to attend Jewish schools, etc. You couldn't do this and you couldn't do that, but life went on. —The Diary of Anne Frank

 Why do you think the Nazis required Jews to wear this yellow star?

_____

Felix Nussbaum, a German-Jewish artist, hid from the Nazis in Belgium but was eventually captured. What do you think his painting *Self-Portrait with Jewish Identity Card* tells us about how he felt during this time?

_____

The Flames of Destruction

The Nazis invaded Poland in 1939 and soon overran other European countries. Their Jewish populations shared the same fate as Germany's Jews. Hitler and the Nazis devised a plan, which they called the "Final Solution," to systematically destroy all Jews within their control. During the six years that the Second World War raged, millions of Jews were taken from their homes and sent to concentration camps where they were ultimately murdered. The destruction of two-thirds of Europe's Jewish population, six million in total, is called the **Holocaust** or **Shoah**. This tragedy, which ended when Germany was defeated by the United States, Britain, and the Soviet Union, had a major effect on Am Yisrael. Jews began to fear for the very existence of the Jewish people in the future. Jews around the world vowed never to let anything like this happen again and to fight against anti-Semitism and prejudice in any form.

Welcome Home

When the United Nations voted in favor of establishing a Jewish state in Palestine in November 1947, Jews around the world burst into joyous celebration. The Zionist dream was finally coming true, and not a moment too soon. After the tragedy of the Holocaust, the desire for a Jewish homeland had taken on more urgency. The Jewish presence in Palestine had been steadily increasing since the late 1800s. During and after the Holocaust, these pioneers helped Jewish refugees make a new home in Palestine. However, many Arabs wanted only an Arab state in Palestine, and their anger increasingly turned to violence against the growing Jewish population. They opposed the United Nations plan, which divided the land between Arabs and Jews. On May 14, 1948, Prime Minister David Ben-Gurion declared Israel's independence. The next day, the neighboring Arab countries attacked Israel. After months of intense fighting, Israel won its War of Independence. The Jewish people finally had a home again in their ancient land.

Talk about It

Why do you think passing on Jewish history is important?

From the Four Corners of the World

Israel's **Law of Return** states that "Every Jew has the right to come to this country…." From the beginning, Israel has welcomed Jewish immigrants who wanted to make *aliyah*, move to Israel, and has even helped whole communities of Jews escape danger in their home countries. As a result, the Jewish population in Israel today is incredibly diverse. Learn about some of the Jewish communities that immigrated to Israel by completing each photo's caption.

Word Bank:
Iraq
Morocco
Soviet Union
Yemen

In 1949, we walked across the desert from our villages in EENYM

_____,

before flying to Israel in a secret mission called Operation Magic Carpet.

About 120,000 of us came to Israel from

QAIR _____

when anti-Jewish violence erupted after Israel became a state.

We fled in secrecy to Israel from the mountains of RCOCMOO.

_____

More than one million Jews made aliyah from the former IVSOTE NNIOU

_____ _____

beginning in 1991 with the collapse of Communism.

Israel Today

From ancient sites to modern cities, holy places to packed beaches, fragrant food markets to vibrant music scenes, modern Israel has something to offer everyone. Imagine that you are planning a trip to Israel. What is your "Israel tourist personality"? Take this quiz to find out.

1. **What will be your family's first day trip?**
   a. A bike trip around Lake Kinneret followed by a hike up a mountain.
   b. A visit to an artists' village where you can make jewelry with gems found in Israel.
   c. A tour of ancient Jerusalem and its Western Wall tunnels.
   d. A day of fun in the sun in Eilat, snorkeling and relaxing on the beach.

2. **For a day of volunteer work, you sign everyone up to:**
   a. Pick vegetables on an Israeli farm and donate them to poor families.
   b. Spend a day in a home for new immigrants, making art projects with children.
   c. Volunteer on an archaeological dig in southern Israel.
   d. Work with a forester planting trees in an Israeli forest.

Jerusalem

3. **Your top choice for an evening out is:**
   a. Catching a Maccabi Tel Aviv soccer game, cheering with Israeli fans.
   b. Hearing popular musicians perform in the ancient Roman theater in Caesarea.
   c. Watching a nighttime show about Jerusalem's history projected onto its ancient walls.
   d. Spending time at an Israeli-style bonfire on the beach.

4. **For a Shabbat to remember, you:**
   a. Attend services at a synagogue whose members are culturally different from you, such as Ethiopian or Bukharan.
   b. Stay in the old city of Safed, touring the city's artists' quarter and beautiful old synagogues.
   c. Savor Shabbat in the Old City of Jerusalem, beginning with a spiritual moment at the Western Wall.
   d. Share a Shabbat meal on a kibbutz, enjoying foods that are mentioned in the Torah, such as pomegranates, dates, or figs.

If you answered . . .

Mostly a's: Action hero—you seek out new and exciting adventures as you explore the country.

Mostly b's: Art lover—from music to art, you appreciate the beauty and talent Israel has to offer.

Mostly c's: History buff—making contact with the past is your top interest.

Mostly d's: Land rover—you love nature and aim to set foot on every inch of the country.

Does this sound like you? How would you describe your Israel tourist personality? _____

_____

_____

Tel Aviv coast

CHAPTER 8

NORTH AMERICAN JEWS:
CHARTING YOUR OWN PATH

Jewish Olympic gymnast Aly Raisman

Becoming Citizens of the World

A Jewish Supreme Court justice, a Passover seder in the White House, Oscar-winning movies about Jewish subjects . . . our ancestors could never have imagined Jewish life in America today, because this kind of involvement in their country's national life was impossible for them. How did we get to this point? As we saw, Jews increasingly took steps to look after their own community, through the Zionist fight for a Jewish state, the founding of Jewish aid organizations, and a growing involvement in American society. American Jews made great advances in politics, the sciences, sports, the arts, and more. Today, Jews are proud citizens of America, Israel, and the world.

Jewish Life in America

In America, you can decide how to balance your Jewish roots and traditions with American ones. When Jewish immigrants first made their way in America, they found that it was easier to be successful if they dropped their Jewish traditions and assimilated, became like other Americans. Some worked on Shabbat for fear of losing their jobs. Some changed their foreign names and clothing so they would blend in. But today, many American Jews have found ways to be true to both their Jewish heritage and their American roots. For example, you may go to public school and have Shabbat on the weekends, or participate in a Jewish mitzvah day by volunteering at a local soup kitchen.

Religious life in America offers many options, too. The Reform, Conservative, and Reconstructionist movements offer a variety of ways to celebrate the Jewish religion, while Orthodox Judaism and Ḥasidism are also flourishing. Women's roles in Judaism have expanded greatly, and in many congregations, women rabbis and cantors stand side by side with men. With all of the choices available, how will you decide what kind of Jewish life you would like to have?

KEY EVENTS

1922	1924	1972	1993
The first public bat mitzvah ceremony in the United States	A new U.S. law strictly limits Jewish immigration	The first female rabbi in the United States is ordained	U.S. Holocaust Memorial Museum opens in Washington D.C.

Your Turn

Ask family members to tell you about an event in Jewish history that has had an impact on their lives or the lives of their parents or grandparents. Collect personal photos and historical images to build a family history photo album, or create an online photo gallery or video documentary.

Multiple Identities

Modern American life can get complex, and there may be many influences that shape who you are. Consider this quote by the first Asian American rabbi and cantor in the United States:

"My father is a Jew and my mother is a Korean Buddhist.... How should Jewish identity be understood, given that *Am Yisrael* reflects the faces of so many nations?... I realized I could no sooner stop being a Jew than I could stop being Korean, or female, or me." —Angela Warnick Buchdahl

How many answers can you give to the question "Who am I?"

I am _____ .

I am _____ .

I am _____ .

A Moment in History

Draw or paste in a photo of an event from Jewish history that you think is relevant to your life today. Then write a caption that explains what it means to you.

_____

_____

Checklist

Give yourself a big check mark for each of the "Your Turn" experiences you have tried.

☐ Design a Torah Ark, page 21

☐ Create a time capsule, page 25

☐ Create a visual metaphor of Jewish American life, page 38

☐ Make a family history photo album, page 47

What other Jewish experiences have you tried for the first time this year?

✔ _____

✔ _____

✔ _____

WORDS TO KNOW

Anti-Semitism Hostility or prejudice against Jews as a religious or ethnic group.

Ashkenazic From the Hebrew *Ashkenaz*, meaning "Germany;" an adjective used to describe Jews and Jewish traditions that originated in Germany and France.

Assimilate Take on the characteristics of the surrounding culture to more easily fit in.

Beit keneset Hebrew term for a synagogue; literally "house of gathering."

Conversos Spanish Jews who were forced to convert to Christianity during the Middle Ages.

Emancipation An eighteenth-century movement in western Europe that granted equal citizenship to Jews and other minority groups.

Holocaust The destruction of six million European Jews by the Nazis and their followers during World War II. Holocaust means "completely burnt offering." It is also referred to as the **Shoah**, Hebrew for "catastrophe."

Kehillah Hebrew for "community." During the Middle Ages, the Jews of France and Germany were permitted to govern their own communities.

Law of Return Israeli law that welcomes Jews from anywhere in the world and gives them the right to immigrate to Israel and become Israeli citizens.

Monotheism The belief in one God.

Sephardic From the Hebrew Sepharad, "Spain;" an adjective used to describe Jews and Jewish traditions that originated in Spain.

Zionism A nineteenth-century movement founded by Theodor Herzl to create a modern Jewish state in the Land of Israel.

Welcome sign at Ben-Gurion International Airport, Tel Aviv, Israel